Th
Deciphered

An Atrahasis Retell as Understood,

Retold and Questioned

by Steven Q

The most complete copy of the Atrahasis tablets on display in the London Museum

The Atrahasis Deciphered

An Atrahasis Retell as Understood,

Retold and Questioned

by Steven Q

COPYRIGHT

Copyright © 2017 by Steven Q

First Edition: 2017
Second Edition 2018

ISBN 978-1-387-20179-2

Published by The Q7 Foundation
Adelaide, South Australia

Email: stevenq7@hotmail.com

All rights reserved. Without limiting the rights under copyright above, no part of this publication may be reproduced, stored or introduced into a retrieval system, or transmitted in any form or by any means (electronic, mechanical, photocopying, recording or otherwise) without the prior written permission of the author or his legal inheritors, except for the use of brief quotations in a book review or scholarly journal.

CONTENTS

INTRODUCTION	1
TABLET 1	10
TABLET 2	41
TABLET 3	49
ACKNOWLEDGEMENTS:	59
PHOTOS AND ILLUSTRATIONS:	60
ABOUT THE AUTHOR:	65

INTRODUCTION

Many are familiar with the Biblical story of Noah's ark, but few are aware of the similarities between the Genesis version and the much older accounts of a great flood. The Atrahasis Epic is one of these accounts. Written on stone tablets in ancient cuneiform text, this story details how and why humans were created, with the addition of a giant flood at the end that was used to destroy them. The copies found of the Atrahasis Epic are believed to have been written around 1,700 BCE (3,700 years ago) and even these tablets seemed to have been copied from an even older version. While the cuneiform tablets of the Atrahasis Epic are mainly fragmented and damaged, there were fortunately a few copies of it discovered, written in both Babylonian and Assyrian cuneiform script. The most complete version of this is on display in the London Museum where the whole Atrahasis story is told over 3 clay tablets.

Not only do parts of the Noah story seemed to have been taken from the Atrahasis Epic, but so does much of the pre-Biblical Babylonian story called the "Enuma Elish" (also known as the "7 tablets of creation"). The Biblical Genesis telling of the flood story dates back to around 540 BCE (around 2,500 years ago) and was said to have been written after Moses led the Israelites out of Babylon, where they'd been captive for 70 years. Logically, we can assume that living amongst the Babylonians for 70 years, the Israelites picked up some of the Babylonian Enuma Elish religion at that time. This influence (or aspects of) may have been incorporated into Moses' written account of creation. The Babylonian, Enuma Elish had its own version of creation and is said to have been written around 1,100 BCE (around 3,100 years ago) nearly 600 years before the Genesis account. It can therefore be assumed that this story was probably modified and partly used in Moses' Genesis.

There is an even older version of an ancient flood known as the "Eridu Genesis" which pre-dates even the Atrahasis. This account is written on a single fragmented tablet and at this stage is the oldest version known, this is also thought to have been copied from yet an even older version. This story is said to be dated at around 2,300-3,000 BCE (around 5,000 years ago) and is believed to focus on a localised flood that did actually occur in the Southern Babylonian region around 2,800 BCE, when the Tigris and Euphrates rivers both flooded. While the Eridu Genesis may be the oldest version of the flood story, I've decided to base my rewrite on the Atrahasis Epic (I may tackle the Eridu Genesis and the Enuma Elish at a later date).

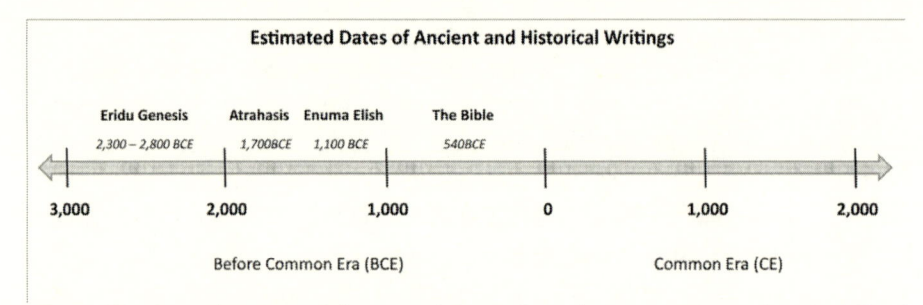

Figure 1 – An estimation of the age of the various documented creation and flood stories. Note that these dates don't necessarily relate to the happenings of the events at the time written as these writings were more likely to have been re-writes or copies of even older documents.

Atrahasis, which literally means "Wise One" or "exceedingly wise" was the king of Shuruppak before the time of the flood and it was said that he walked with the gods. It's not entirely clear if Atrahasis himself originally wrote the creation story as dictated by the gods of the time, or he employed a scribe to write it for him based on information he'd received from them. Atrahasis also included his own experiences with the gods and of the flood in his epic. As noted above, the original Atrahasis story of creation was said to have been written before the occurrence of the flood and the complete epic was constantly re-written until around 500 BCE.

What follows in my interpretation of the Atrahasis Epic is what I believe to be a more probable account of creation and the great flood. My version of the story suggests that the gods were merely technologically advanced humanoid beings, probably not much more advanced than we humans are today. My understanding is that advanced, possibly, alien modifications were performed on primitive Earth primates in the distant past. These ancient gods not only created the human race, but also influenced everything that the human race has done since then. There's no denying that a catastrophic global flood struck our planet, or parts of it, 12,000 or so years ago as we left the ice age. The question is, did it occur as told in the Biblical Genesis? The concept of the animals of the world taking a trip to the ark, marching two by two, in loving couples to patiently wait out the storm and the "flood of floods" in a little sealed boat with Noah and his family for 40 days and 40 nights, seems ludicrous with what we know today.

Did the whole world really succumb to a deluge that covered the highest peaks of the highest mountains as told in Genesis? Keep in mind that the Mount Everest summit is slightly less than 9km above sea level. For the peak of this mountain to be covered with water you'd need a phenomenal amount of rain. It's estimated that the amount of water in the oceans, seas, glaziers, lakes and rivers around the world is slightly less than 1.5 Billion Cubic Kilometres. If all mountains were to be covered, the global water level would need to rise enough to cover Mount Everest (a 9km rise). For this to happen, it's estimated that an "additional" 5 Billion Cubic Kilometres of water at least, would be needed! So, if the Noah story is believed to be correct, where did all this extra water come from? If this could be answered, the next question would be, if it took 40 days to drain this abundance of water, where did it all go? Another question is, how did all the animals get to the ark in time? The kangaroos and koalas would have had quite a swim from Australia. It's also obvious that the unicorns and dragons didn't make it to the safety of the floating zoo before its departure. The whole story is nice to read to kids, but logic dictates it couldn't have happened.

Figure 2 – The Biblical depiction of Noah herding the animals of the world into the ark.

As much as the Genesis account probably isn't to be taken literally, the question still stands, how can there still be evidence and flood residue all over the world indicating that there was a global deluge? Many ancient writings all over the world mention floods, some of a global catastrophe, some of a more localized event. Regardless of this, something calamitous must have occurred to have been documented by the past civilizations of the world; this was by them, deemed important enough to record for future generations so not to be forgotten. There are plenty of theories about what happened, if it was indeed a global event. It may have been caused by the slip of an ice sheet into the sea at Antarctica which created a 1 to 2km high tsunami over the surface of the Earth from the South Pole, a pole shift or global flip, or even a giant meteorite hitting the Pacific Ocean. We aren't really sure, but it's possible that one or even all of these events happened at different times in the past.

As previously mentioned, I've rewritten the story with an understanding that the gods were probably a visiting alien humanoid race, with an agenda. Questions are: Were they here to exploit the mineral wealth of the planet? Were they possibly marooned, or were they hiding from other alien pursuers and using Earth as their base? Regardless of these questions, the way the original story was written, suggests that the humans of this time were not technologically advanced enough to understand the motives and doings of these "gods" and the texts were simplistically written as such. It could also possibly be that the story was deliberately written in a basic way to ensure an understanding by all different language cultures of the time. There's also the possibility that mistakes were made in the rewrites and the story gradually changed over the years as it was retold and rewritten onto fresh tablets.

Whichever way you look at it, someone more advanced than us was once living on Earth thousands of years ago. Whether you think it was an advanced human race or aliens, we're still confronted with questions like, who built the Baalbek Platform, and for what? Some of the ancient monolithic stones in this platform weigh between 1,200 and 2,000 tons each and they were carted up from a quarry nearly a kilometre away! We know this, as the constructors of the platform left a few of these giant stones at the quarry and they're still there! With all the technological wonders we have today, we still have no means to transport stones of that size, and have even extreme difficulty moving a 50 ton stone. So, how and why was the platform constructed and by who? It was obviously not built by the Romans as history books tell us, though was honoured and seen by them to be important as they built their "Temple of Jupiter" on top of the deserted platform nearly 2,000 years ago. With the platform recently estimated to be possibly 12,000 or even 20,000 years old it's not surprising that after visiting the Baalbek Platform you walk away thinking that somehow or another, historians have obviously got it all wrong.

Figure 3 - Ruins of the Temple of Jupiter showing the large monolithic stones forming the Baalbek Platform.

Figure 4 – The lone, unused megalith stone left in the quarry a kilometre away from the platform. The pillars from the Temple of Jupiter can be clearly seen in the background.

Special Thanks to the Original Translators

My version of the Atrahasis story that follows has been formulated after reading many translations of the original cuneiform text. By taking the commonalities from all of these versions, I managed to form the basic story as I understand it (taking the standpoint that the Atrahasis story was real and not a mythical work of fiction). Due to this, you'll find that this story version does not favour any particular translation and is more of a mixture of them all. Where parts of the original Atrahasis Epic were missing or damaged on the tablets, some translators used sections of stories (from other tablets) that shared commonalities or had over-lapping story areas to help fill in the gaps, which I have also used. While none of Zecharia Sitchin's material has been used in my version, I still have great admiration for much of his work and it's thanks to him, that an interest in the ancient cuneiform stories was stirred up.

None of this would have been possible without the efforts of the many brilliant and dedicated people, who spent mind numbing amounts of time working out what was written on the original cuneiform tablets and then translating them into verse English. I feel it's only right to acknowledge and give special thanks to George Smith, Heinrich Zimmern, Wilfred Lambert, Alan Millard, Benjamin Foster, Stephanie Dalley and the many, many others who translated the cuneiform text. Due to the technology of today, a big thank you for the work of the many scholars who freely offered their own translations and insights on the Internet for all to read. These Internet translations are partly due to the fantastic offerings of people like John Halloran with his online "Sumerian Lexicon" dictionary.

My Recommended Method on How to Read this Version

I've tried to keep as much of the original translated dialogue in my story as possible, which was difficult. While the spoken dialogue in quotes may seem to be lengthy in some places, this (or an approximation of) was what was apparently said, or what I felt was meant. The story at some stages, may also seem to have a combination of old style English mixed with modern language, this is deliberate and was necessary to keep the context of what I understand happened and the story intact. After each section I've added footnotes in numerical order. These are important and will either add extra information, an elaboration, or my thoughts and observations. The large numbers in brackets are deliberately made this big for easy access and matching to the footnotes after reading the section.

The best method to read this story is to first read each section of the tablet translations in their entirety, skipping over the bracketed numbers. After the section of the story has been understood, the footnotes should then be read, thus allowing the reader to revisit the bracketed footnote number in the story section for better understanding of the context, if needed. In doing this, understanding the points made after following the continuity of the story section will hopefully allow it to make more sense by elaboration.

Figure 5 - The most complete copy of the Atrahasis tablets on display in the London Museum.

TABLET 1

The Lower Igigi Gods Complain and Revolt

Long ago before humans roamed the Earth, the lesser gods (known as the Igigi) bore the brunt of the work, doing all the heavy laborious tasks that needed to be done. They weren't happy, were miserable and constantly complained to the higher gods (known as the Anunna gods or Anunnaki) that their work was heavy and troublesome. The higher ruling Anunnaki gods that controlled the Igigi gods at that time were: King Anu, the ruling Anunnaki god and father to the higher gods, his son the councillor warrior, Enlil, their chief officer Ninurta (a son of Enlil) and the god Ennugi who was the controller of the canals.

The gods decided to rearrange the management positions on Earth. So, to properly divide up the lands and ruling positions between the king's sons, the Anunnaki gods decided that lots should be drawn amongst themselves. With the result of the lots cast, after King Anu, the father of the controlling gods had returned to his sky home in Heaven *(1)*, Enlil the warrior was given charge of the land and the minor gods upon it. Control of the sea and fresh waters was given to Enlil's wise half-brother Enki, known by the other gods as the far sighted one.

Figure 6 – The cuneiform symbol used in the texts for the king and father god Anu.

Figure 7 – Enlil (on the left) and his wife Ninlil. The original mural is on display in the Louvre in Paris.

Figure 8 – The Adda Seal in the British Museum. Far left is Inanna depicted as a pilot with weapons, followed by her twin brother Utu digging in the mountain. Enki is shown with rivers of fish flowing over him with his chief minister Usimu behind him.

When their father Anu had returned to his heavenly home and with the new management team in place, the Anunnaki gods returned to the lower areas of the Earth known as the Abzu *(2)* and proceeded to overwork the poor Igigi gods as they'd done before. In the Abzu, the Igigi were forced to dig canals to run water to barren areas of land, they also dug out the Tigris and Euphrates water ways. *(3)* In the depths of the Abzu they raised mountains of soil and worked under the ground. *(4)* The Igigi counted 40 years *(5)* that they'd been worked hard day and night and they grumbled constantly amongst themselves about all the masses of soil that they'd excavated.

1. *Heaven seems to have been situated in the air, or "moving up in the air" was needed to reach it. However, it is possible that it may have been a mountain retreat or a high-up residence that looked down on the workers below.*
2. *The Abzu is described as the lower lands or underworld, however, from my own and other people's research I feel it may refer to the lands that fall below the equator in Africa. Keeping this in mind though, according to the Sumerian Lexicon (dictionary) by John Halloran, in this context Ab+Zu means "the sentient sea" or "the sea personified as a god" (aba/ab = "sea" + zu = "to know"). This is probably why Enki was referred to as "god of the sea" and this title is later echoed in Greek and Roman cultures where he was referred by them as the gods Poseidon and Neptune respectively. However, "god of the sea" in the depths of the African "Abzu"? This doesn't really make sense to me as if this is the case, how could the Igigi dig mountains of earth in the sea? As this would mean that they were working underwater! A possible explanation of this is the evidence of an enormous inland fresh water sea that seems to have once existing in Africa, at what's known today as the Okavango Delta (more on this later, see Figures 9, 10 & 11). In addition to this, if we consider that deep down in Africa the ancient indigenous*

people of Southern Africa referred to themselves (and also when they initially introduced themselves to early Europeans) as the "Zulu" people. Again, considering the context of the word and used as an adjective with a noun, the Sumerian Lexicon dictionary demonstrates that Zulu can be broken down to Zu = Wisdom, Knowledge and the word Lu = Man, Men, People or Sheep (somehow another, I don't think in this case it means sheep). Basically then, the word "Zulu" literally means "Intelligent people" or "Wise men".

3. *The waterways of the Tigris and Euphrates river systems are still actively used today, with some of the canals reported to indeed be extremely ancient. Remnants of the canals that were channelled in the Abzu also remain, with the ancient contours gouged into the Earth still visible as evidence of an advanced civilization that once was. These ancient canals can be viewed on Google Earth running from the Okavango Delta in Botswana, Southern Africa, which once must have been an enormous inland lake or sea (Google Earth, Latitude and Longitudes -19.824346 21.714989). The canals all seem to end abruptly at where the boundary of the huge inland lake or sea must have once been and they would have been used to transport water to crops that were to feed possibly millions or even billions of Igigi and later human workers.*

Figure 9 – Okavango Delta. Here we can see the remnants of an enormous inland lake with the remains of the ancient canals visible on the left. The size of this once huge lake can be determined by the obvious abrupt ending of the canals which originally was the lake's or inland sea's perimeter.

Figure 10 - A close-up of the ancient canals reveals that they are perfectly straight with little deviation, which rules out the possibility of them being a natural occurrence. The canals all run from East to West with an off-set of around 10 degrees. This off-set may indicate a slight shift of the Earth on its axis many, many years ago and the canals may have originally been built to run from East to West before this axis shift occurred.

Figure 11 – From a further close-up, the uniformity of the canals can clearly be seen. The canals are equally spaced apart at around 1.5kms with the width of each canal being around 250 metres. The combined length of these canals equates to thousands of kilometres of irrigation which would have taken many years to dig.

4. *Logic dictates that the mountains of soil created were probably due to the earth being removed from digging under the ground. From this it can further be assumed that some sort of mining was being done in the area.*
5. *There seems to be some discrepancy here with some scholars translating the 40 years that I've used in my version as 3600 years, or 40 years too much. If it's 40 years too much, I'm wondering "too much" of what? Did the Igigi possibly have a contract with the Anunnaki and it was exceeded by 40 years?*

The Uprising of the Igigi Gods

In the end, the Igigi couldn't take it anymore and amongst them decided to go pay their leader Enlil a visit and have a serious chat with him to see if he could make life a little easier for them. The orchestrator of the uprising *(1)* had the Igigi all excited and worked up by shouting "let's take Enlil from his home and start war cries to initiate a battle with the higher controlling gods!" The unhappy Igigi listened attentively to his speech, agreed and in protest, set fire to their tools, picks, spades and work baskets. The mob gathered and off they all went to the gate of Enlil's home chanting around the Ekur, which was the name of Enlil's mountain retreat. It was night, half-way through the Igigi's night-shift and Enlil's property was totally surrounded. Enlil was unaware of what was going on as he was fast asleep. Luckily for him, his gatekeeper Kalkal was awake, and quickly closed and locked the main gate *(2)* then guarded it before the Igigi mob could get onto the property. Seeing that the gate was now safely locked, Kalkal woke up Enlil's chief officer Nusku and the two of them listened to the noise and chanting of the Igigi rebels on the other side of the gate. "I reckon I'd better go wake Enlil up", said Nusku and off he hurried and did just that. "My Lord Enlil, wake up!" said Nusku, "Your house is surrounded by Igigi rabble and they're not happy, it looks like they're getting ready to battle with you".

Enlil acted quickly and organised weapons to be brought to his home. Raising his voice, he spoke to Nusku saying "Nusku, bar your door and take up your weapons in front of me". Nusku did as he was told and stood with weapon in hand in front of Enlil barring the gate. Turning back to Enlil, he noticed his master's fear and said, "Enlil, my Lord, your face is as white as a tamarisk bush, why do you fear your own off-spring? *(3)* Why don't you call your father Anu to give you a hand in dealing with this situation and maybe also send message to your brother Enki to back you up?" *(4)* So Enlil did just that, he contacted his father Anu and his brother Enki to help sort out the confronting situation and fortunately for him, they both came. Anu, king of the sky and Enki, king of the waters and the Lower Abzu lands both arrived. With the support of his father and brother, Enlil stood up to make his case. He approached both of them asking, "Is it me that they've risen against? With my own eyes I witness this Igigi rabble surrounding my home in such a way that I'm actually wondering if maybe I should indeed battle them."

1. At this point it isn't revealed that the ring-leader of the revolt was not an Igigi worker but a younger Anunnaki god by the name of Geshtu. Geshtu was probably a supervisor or manager of the worker gods.
2. The main gate at Enlil's residence seems to have just been the entrance to his property (known as the Ekur, which I'd assume was walled or separated from the outside somehow). It would seem that Kalkal only locked the property gate and not the actual gate for Enlil's home as there was movement from house to house in the enclosure while the Igigi rebels were outside (weapons collected, Nusku told to bar his door, etc).
3. This is an interesting bit, nearly all of the Atrahasis translations I've read seem to indicate that the Igigi were the children of Enlil. As the story unfolded, I came to the conclusion that the Anunna gods or Anunnaki could not reproduce in the traditional way and cloning may have been their chosen or only way of reproducing (more explanation on this later as the story unfolds).
4. I'd assume that the property was walled and there may have been another entrance to it, or maybe access was possible from the air. Otherwise, how would Enlil be able to contact and receive his father and brother while the Igigi were gathering at his gate and surrounding his property? Not only this, what form of communication would have been used to contact his family members while he was trapped inside the Ekur enclosure?

The Anunnaki Gods Send a Negotiator

Anu then turned to his son and said, "Enlil, why don't you send Nusku your chief officer to speak with them and find out the reason why they're so upset and have surrounded your home?" Liking the idea, Enlil turned and spoke to Nusku saying, "Nusku, open the door, take your weapon and go out and represent me. However, show some respect and bow before you address them. Say to the Igigi that their king, King Anu, their warrior leader, Enlil, their chief officer, Ninurta and their bailiff, Ennugi have sent you to ask who is in charge of this Igigi mob and the declaration of war against me by surrounding my home?" *(1)*

So the concerned Nusku opened the door and with his weapon in hand nervously went into the assembly of the lower Igigi gods. He bowed before them and delivered Enlil's message. The leader of the Igigi revolt sprung up and answered the question saying, "Every one of us gods has declared war! We've got to put a stop to the digging, it's killing us! The work is too heavy, too hard and too much, so every one of us gods has agreed to stop work and complain together in unison to Enlil." After the Igigi revolt leader had finished stating their reasons, Nusku nodded, took his weapon and reported the Igigi's sad story in full detail back to Enlil. Enlil listened to all that Nusku had to say and tears were flowing down his face. *(2)* Upset with the Igigi's rejection, Enlil then spoke to Anu, his father the warrior king, saying, "Mighty Anu, let me return with you to heaven in the sky and you take control of the situation and demonstrate your strength while the rest of us Anunnaki sit with you. Call up one of the rebellious gods and kill him as an example to the others".

Annoyed, Anu jumped up and abruptly answered, "Can you really blame them? Their work was extremely difficult and every day we could hear their cries of pain as they laboured and we chose to ignore them! In all fairness, they have every right to complain to their ruler Enlil and approach his house".

1. *I found it strange that in all the translations of the Atrahasis I've read that Enki wasn't mentioned here. It's already been established that Enki being of similar royal status to Enlil and*

was definitely there, however, Enlil mentions the other gods to Nusku, but failed to include Enki. Could it be due to Enki not having a military position, or perhaps Enki choosing not to let the Igigi know he was there, or was this possibly the onset to the sibling rivalry?
2. *All translations I've read seem to indicate that Enlil had a good cry. To be honest with you, I don't swallow this. Enlil, the great warrior crying? Regardless of whether he's scared or feels rejected, I still can't see how this great warrior goes crying to daddy that he wants to come home, or that he's upset that the Igigi are having a hard time.*

The Creation of Man and the Introduction of Nintu

Enlil wasn't very happy with his father's comments. Deep in thought, Enki then spoke up, addressing his father, brother and other gods he said, "I agree, why are we blaming them? They are indeed over-worked and it's true we did ignore their constant cries whilst they laboured."*(1)* Turning to his father he said, "I believe there is an answer to this problem noble King Anu. Call our wise sister the birth goddess Nintu and ask her to join us, she can organize the birth of a mortal humanoid slave that can do the heavy labour of the lower Igigi gods". *(2)*

Later, when the birth goddess, Nintu, who was in charge of the surrogate womb goddesses and midwives had joined them, Enki asked her, "Are you willing to also be the birth goddess of mankind? *(3)* We need you and your surrogate womb goddesses to help create a humanoid slave to bear the labour of the lower Igigi worker gods".

1. *If anything, your brother sucking up and agreeing with daddy when you've just been told off by him would make anyone angry. Frankly, I don't think this was a good move by Enki to agree with his father against Enlil in this condescending way. Enki should have maybe rather introduced his solution in*

agreement to his father without adding to Enlil's reprimanding, especially considering that his brother is a great warrior and next in charge after Anu.
2. *I'm guessing that Enki had been preparing for the right occasion of making a team of slaves for a while and he just seized this opportunity of convenience to make his "helpful" suggestion.*
3. *Nintu seems to have many names and is the half-sister to both Enki and Enlil. I chose to remain with the name Nintu all the way through the story to avoid confusion. Some of the translated versions of the texts were confusing, as her name not only changed depending on her position held at that time, but sometimes it changed without explanation. Nintu was also known as the "Birth Goddess", not to be mixed up with one of the "Womb Goddesses" which she is called sometimes in the original translations when she chose to also take up the birthing responsibility. Regarding the "Womb Goddesses", you'll also notice I've added the word surrogate in some places to elaborate on their position and function as baby-incubators, which is quite obviously what they were. In addition to this, the "also" part of Enki saying to Nintu "Are you willing to 'also' be the birth goddess of mankind?" gets me thinking. Also to what? Does this mean that she was birth goddess to the Igigi as well? Were the Igigi perhaps just clones created from Enlil's DNA brought into the world through the womb goddesses? This is indeed a possibility, as why did Nusku question Enlil about fearing his own off-spring?*

Figure 12 – Ancient statuette of Nintu on display in the University of Chicago.

Figure 13 – Inanna, Queen of the Night. Known as the "Burney Relief". Found in the British Museum.

Nintu Responds to Enki's Proposition

Nintu listened attentively to Enki's question and facing the gods answered, "It's not proper, nor my place to create a humanoid man, as it's outside my jurisdiction. That area is Enki's. I don't mind assisting Enki making a co-worker, but I'm definitely not helping him make a slave!" *(1)* Forcefully, Nintu then added, "This has to be Enki's work and he will be totally responsible for it. If Enki needs me to assist, he will need to provide a pure and clean area to work in. If he brings me a being of the Earth and the essence of the slaughtered Igigi rebel leader I will assist with the manufacturing of this new humanoid being. *(2)* With Enki's help, I'll combine like clay the essence of both the executed Anunnaki leader of the Igigi rebels and that of the creature of the Earth to form a new co-worker being." *(3)*

Enki then answered, "Wise Nintu, mother of all the gods *(4)*, your wisdom is noted and shall always be remembered. On the first, seventh and fifteenth of the month I shall establish a purified area *(5)*, the essence of the executed rebel Annunaki god *(6)* who led the Igigi rebellion and a being of the Earth shall be provided". Facing the gods Enki then added, "Let the Anunnaki gods who assist and their equipment be cleansed and washed to ensure that there is no contamination. Nintu can then combine the essence of both the Earth being and the executed Anunnaki god by making it into one, mixed as like clay. The Anunnaki god and the being of the Earth will then be mixed together permanently and from then on we will hear the drumming of its heartbeat forever after in this new created being. Let the spirit *(7)* of the perished god also enter into this new being, so not to be forgotten".

> 1. *Good for you Nintu! That's what we like to hear. Nintu made it quite clear that the position of making a being was not hers, but Enki's, and if he was making slaves she wasn't interested in helping. I've also assumed from here that Enki was the geneticist and Nintu didn't mind assisting him, but couldn't (or wouldn't) create a new being on her own. Enki obviously*

needed Nintu for access to her womb goddesses or surrogates, so the two of them had to work together.

2. *I've used the word "essence" throughout my adaptation of the story to describe what appears to be the DNA of both the Anunnaki god and the hominid "Being of the Earth" (not a "being" created of earth). I feel that an upright walking hominid primate was wandering around on Earth at the time and its DNA was merged with that of the Anunnaki's to create the new being. Without going into too much detail here, primates have 48 chromosomes (humans are not primates!) humans have 46 chromosomes which separates them from the primate family line. When primate and human chromosomes are scrutinised comparatively, there's an "obvious" fusion of a primate's 2+3 chromosome on both strands which somehow another became the human chromosome 2 (bringing humans down to 46 chromosomes from a primate's 48). If a primate's 2+3 chromosomes from both parents were indeed fused together this would create a 46 chromosome structure (or 23 base pairs). This may have been what was done at a genetic level to convert our primate ancestor's DNA into a DNA that was compatible with another 46 chromosome species, which I'd assume was the Anunnaki or Igigi race. If you're interested in reading more about this, or looking for a better, more detailed explanation, get hold of Lloyd Pye's book "Intervention Theory Essentials" or hunt down his video "Everything you know is wrong" on YouTube.*

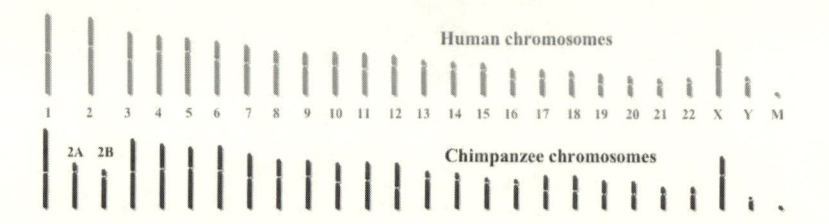

Figure 14 – Above we have the chromosomes of both human and the chimpanzee of the primate family. The chimpanzee's chromosomes 2+3 are being shown as 2A+2B in the illustration to demonstrate how the rest of the chromosomes line up exactly. Chimpanzees are our nearest relations sharing about 98.9% of their DNA with humans.

3. While the translated texts all seem to indicate that the essence of the executed Igigi rebel and the creature of the Earth were mixed into a clay, I think that this wasn't meant to be taken literally. Mixing "like" a clay seemed more appropriate to me and more probable than making humans from clay. I believe that mixing the essence of both species like clay was used to indicate that once mixed there was no separation of the DNAs as it would then be an independent being from both contributing sources.

4. Nintu is addressed by Enki in all translated versions I've read as "Mother of 'all' the gods" which I think is another point leaning towards her being the head of the womb goddesses. This then insinuates that either "all" the gods were being cloned from source DNA, or that they were being born from surrogate mothers and weren't born by what we consider natural births.

5. I'm not sure of what the significance of the 1st, 7th and 15th of the month is, however, there's much in the scripts that seems to indicate that the Lunar month was used extensively, which is 28 days. This may be the reason we use seven days as our week lengths (with a further question of why 15 was used for

the last day and not 14). Enki's purified area I'm guessing was either his laboratory or a work area at his home.

6. *Here it seems that Enlil got his way and the rebel Igigi leader was to be executed and his DNA used. Also, we're told that the Igigi rebel leader was from the ruling Anunnaki family. This would mean that he would have been a higher god and not a lowly Igigi worker as we were led to initially assume. Does that mean that we humans originate from an Anunnaki trouble maker? At this stage of the story there's still no mention of the slaughtered god's name and this seems to be the case in all versions of the translated texts I've examined.*

7. *It's interesting here that the "spirit" of the executed Anunnaki leader of the Igigi rebel was mentioned. Some translations of the cuneiform texts seem to indicate the inclusion of the spirit into the new creation, while others seem to call it the dead god's ghost. Whichever way you choose to see it, the indication of a spiritual presence living inside both the gods and new human template, meant that the original ancient author believed that the spirit was essentially the identity of the living person. This would strongly indicate the belief in an immortal soul and a further belief in reincarnation. It can be assumed from this, that the original manufacturers of the first human had a choice. Instead of making their new worker a genetically manufactured humanoid machine (which many assume the grey aliens to be) this new being had the inclusion of an immortal soul.*

The First Source Being and the First Humans are Created

Seeing this as a solution to their problems, all the gods in the great Anunnaki assembly agreed to the procedure. And so, on the first, seventh and fifteenth days, Enki and Nintu participated in a purification washing of both themselves and their work area. The young and intelligent rebel Anunnaki god known by the name of Geshtu *(1)*, the inspiration behind the Igigi rebellion, was executed and his essence mixed with an Earth being's, like clay. The gods all waited in anticipation for the drumbeat of the newly created being's heart and as suggested by Enki, the spirit of the slaughtered Anunnaki god entered it. Upon this, Nintu then proclaimed that with both the heartbeat and the incorporation of the spirit into the new being, it was now alive. *(2)* After this, the greater controlling Igigi gods were gathered and saliva was collected from each of them. *(3)* Each of the high ranking Igigi gods' genetic identities in the saliva was then combined with the essence of the newly created being's, thus creating additional genetic variations for further living human hybrids. *(4)*

Nintu then faced and addressed the gods saying, "I have done the work that you have ordered me to do. You have sacrificed an Anunnaki god and his intelligence and I have relieved you of your hard work. I've now placed your workload onto this being and it is understood that it is to be a co-worker, not a slave! The gift of life I may have given to this new being, but also something to complain about, as it now has to bear the burden of the lesser gods. I have only freed the lesser Igigi gods back to the time before the greater Anunnaki gods forced the hard labour upon them."

All the gods listened carefully to Nintu's speech and the Igigi gods, now freed, fell down on their knees and kissed Nintu's feet saying, "We used to call you Mami *(5)*, but now you shall always be known to us as Belet-kala-ili, Mistress-of-all-the-gods"

> 1. *This is the first time we get to know the actual name of the executed rebel god. Many of the translated texts I've read seem to indicate that the slaughtered god's name was Aw-ilu. The word Aw-ilu translated actually relates to the class of the people, that being royalty and the higher ruling classes of the*

Anunnaki gods. So, Aw-ilu was not the actual name of the young executed god, but the title of his Anunnaki status. While this god's social status was Aw-ilu, his actual name was Geshtu and he was known as "a young and intelligent god".
2. Nintu only proclaimed that the new being was alive when the spirit entered the being's body. My understanding of this is that the incorporation of the spirit into the being was an important attribute for it to be considered "alive". I assume that this template being was the first of the 46 chromosome beings which was created entirely to be a base source of DNA for a further species. The DNA from this new being (complete with soul) was then combined with DNA gathered from the saliva donated by the higher Igigi gods, which then created even more DNA diversity. If the Igigi were all male, this also indicates that the new being may have been either androgynous or female as both sexes were then separated in the actual final creation of the humans (as seen later). The final Igigi and new-being hybrids were then carried to term by the womb goddesses further mentioned in the story.
3. The high ranking Igigi gods where the saliva was collected from may have been Anunnaki gods, however, all texts seem to emphasize that they were Igigi not Anunnaki. This would then mean that no royal blood or DNA was added to the new being's, other than that of the initially executed god Geshtu. In the actual translated texts, it was stressed that the higher ranking Igigi gods each spat into the mix, with research I discovered that saliva is indeed an excellent source for preserving DNA and is teeming with it.
4. Here I added "genetic variations" as this was my understanding of what occurred. The clay and mud stories just seemed a little far-fetched to me, and if I was to take the story seriously I had to improvise to make sense of it all. The introductions of the higher Igigi's DNA from their saliva,

mixed with the first hybrid's DNA would give an amount of DNA diversity for healthy reproduction of the new species of human. If this is then considered, the human species has three-quarters of the gods DNA and only one quarter from the "beings of the Earth" which I assume were the 48 chromosome primates available at that time. This would also suggest that despite the slight chromosome differential between the gods and Earth primates, there was probably an even more ancient genetic connection between the primates and Anunnaki that made the Anunnaki genetic tampering possible.

5. *Mami was one of Nintu's many names that she was known by, depending on her position taken at that time and who was addressing her. Nintu was re-titled by the Igigi from Mami which meant "Lady of Birth" to Belet-kala-ili meaning "Mistress of 'all' the gods". From the Igigi's point of view, Nintu had now incorporated more species of beings under her motherly title. It's easy to see from here that the word Mami is similar to the words Mammy or Mamma used by today's infants in many cultures to address their mothers. I'd assume that these designative words stem from Nintu's Birth goddess title.*

The First Humans are Created

With the creation of the new being, Enki and Nintu then went into the "Room of Fate" where the womb goddesses had assembled to be the surrogates for the new species. Enki continued to mix the essence of the new being with that of the high ranking Igigi's while Nintu watched and recited an incantation. *(1)* After she'd finished, she separated the completed mixture into fourteen parts and placed seven parts on the right and the other seven on the left. Nintu then separated the two sets of seven with a mud brick into male and female groups. *(2)* With a sharp implement made from a reed, Nintu split open the umbilical cord and removed the embryos from each of them. *(3)* With the seven male and seven female embryos Nintu then called to the surrogate mothers which she'd named "seven and seven" and inserted each of them into their wombs. *(4)* Enki on Nintu's request led the seven surrogate mothers carrying the females to one room and the other seven surrogate mothers carrying the males to another. *(5)*

1. *I have no idea what Nintu's incantation was. Maybe she was humming a song while she worked, or maybe it was a significant part of the procedure like a magical blessing or vibratory noise that needed to be made. However, it seems to be significant as it was mentioned in all translations I've come across.*
2. *The significance of the "mud brick" as a separator is not clear and I presumed this meant separating the male and female test tube babies into either different rooms separated by a brick wall, or maybe separating the two different sexes into different buildings.*
3. *This was unclear in all the translations I came across, while the sharp implement was clear, the rest wasn't. Also, much of the tablet's text is fragmented or missing lines here, so some of the sources of the translations I'd found had added the missing parts of the story from other translated texts like "The Epic of Gilgamesh" to fill in the gaps. The actual procedure is also mentioned further in the story, however, sadly this is also mostly damaged.*
4. *This is pretty clear in other cuneiform text stories, but again most of the procedure is unfortunately missing from the original Atrahasis tablets due to damage. Other tellings of the story on Assyrian or Babylonian tablets definitely seem to indicate that the womb goddesses were used to gestate the new human babies. The Embryos must have somehow been grown*

from the final DNA mixes. These embryos would then have been moved into the surrogate mother's uteruses in a similar way to how IVF treatment is performed today.
5. *This could even have been different buildings as Nintu makes it clear later that males and females were to be kept separate from each other, until deemed mature enough to breed and take care of themselves.*

Nintu Presents Her Conditions for Male and Female Pairing

Nintu then addressed the gods with her rules, "In the house where a surrogate womb goddess is about to give birth, she shall be looked after in the building for seven days after. I Nintu, the birth goddess, shall be honoured to be in the house at the time that a surrogate mother gives birth to her baby. The duty of cutting the umbilical cord will be that of the mothers".

Nintu continued, saying, "With time, we will observe the humans as they mature and as a male becomes of age it will be noticed by the beard appearing on his cheek and he should then find and join with a woman of his own choice. When a female grows into a woman, it will be noticed by the growth of her bosoms, with this she should also then seek out and join with a male of her choosing. *(1)* There in the gardens and streets they will choose each other as mates and as husband and wife they will be happy and joyful together as a couple". *(2)*

1. *Nintu makes it clear that when a woman and man reach puberty they would be encouraged to take a life mate. From this we can deduce that in doing so they could then self-procreate without the need of a birth goddess, and the human species' numbers would continue to grow exponentially without Anunnaki intervention.*
2. *Nintu again makes it quite clear that both the male and female should choose each other and not be forced into wedlock. She*

emphasised that if they had both chosen each other they would then be happy together. Whether this means that there'd be a larger amount of off-spring from the couple due to it being a more loving union, or there was a reason for the pair's choice in each other that may involve better breeding compatibility, maybe due to pheromonal influence or a "survival of the fittest" type scenario.

The First Surrogate Child is Born

After a time, the surrogate womb goddess mothers were brought together with Nintu. The months were counted and the expecting tenth month *(1)* was called "the term of fates". On this tenth month, Nintu approached the first of the surrogate mothers and preformed a medical procedure to open her womb. With her face covered, Nintu then took her midwife belt and carefully girdled the expecting mother and started to perform her midwifery duty. *(2)* As Nintu carefully begun removing the baby from the first womb goddess she was happy and excited, her face was beaming and joyful. After the mother had cut the umbilical cord, Nintu blessed the child and wrote down the details of the child in the building's registry. *(3)*

Figure 15 – This cylinder seal image is known as the Shu-ilishus cylinder seal, dated from around 2,000 BCE and it is on display in the Louvre museum in Paris. The image clearly shows Nintu (recognised by her dress) holding up a child before two other gods.

Holding up the child, Nintu proudly addressed the gods saying, "I am the one who has created this child, my hands have made it. From now on, let the midwives rejoice and celebrate in the birthing house like a priestess when the pregnant woman gives birth. Whenever a midwife delivers a baby, both her and the birthing woman should rest for nine days and both should be honoured together. After time, when the male and female infants have matured to adulthood and have chosen each other, I the birth goddess, Nintu shall then lay down a linen cloth and in their house, Inanna will celebrate the husband and wife relationship. *(4)* In the new wife's father's home there will be a wedding celebration that shall last for nine days. On the fifteenth day after the wedding, Inanna, who should then be called by the couple, Ishtar, shall visit with myself, as the birth goddess. Both Inanna and I will deliver our blessing to the couple which shall from that point in time be known as the "fixed time of their fate". *(5)*

1. *It's stressed in all translations I've read that the woman stays pregnant for 10 months not nine. When you consider that a*

lunar month is again used here of 28 days and not the months we use today of 31 days, the time of a woman's pregnancy does indeed add up to "exactly" 10 lunar months.

2. *It's clear here a complex medical procedure was used to remove the baby from the surrogate host. A caesarean-section would have been performed and the reason why Nintu wore a mask, presumably a medical mask. I'm not quite sure the significance of girdling the surrogate mother or womb goddess with a midwife belt was though.*

3. *In the original texts, after the baby was born, Nintu wrote a symbol in some sort of meal powder. I can only guess that she wrote the baby's name and the time of its birth in a type of register and indicated this in my interpretation.*

4. *Here we move forward to when the new human male and female have chosen each other. Nintu indicates that she will set up their bed for them to consummate their husband and wife marriage union.*

5. *It seems that the tradition of the father of the bride holding the marriage celebration may have stemmed from here. The introduction of Inanna onto the scene and her then being known as Ishtar (goddess of love) by the couple after 15 days, indicates that both Inanna and Nintu expected the new bride to be pregnant. The arrival of the two goddesses would indicate that some sort of inspection of the new bride was to be done, possibly to verify her pregnancy and to assist if she wasn't. The "fixed time of their fate" was probably the time of conception noted for the couple and when the goddesses would deliver their blessings.*

The Humans Reproduce and Enlil Introduces a Plague

Enlil was happy with Enki and Nintu's work as the new humans grew quickly and when they reached adulthood they happily took up tools, making new picks, spades and work tools for themselves. Without complaint, they dug new canals and irrigational systems to grow crops to feed both the gods and themselves. The added bonus was that they could also now happily reproduce without any assistance from the gods or birth goddesses.

After around 1,200 *(1)* years had passed, the number of humans in the area had increased dramatically and there were many of them in the small area of land. Enlil was getting a little annoyed with the noise that these humans were making and commented that the land bellowed like a bull which was upsetting him. In addition to the racket, some of the Igigi were taking the genetically compatible female humans as their wives and having children with them. *(2)* Enlil formed a council and addressed the other gods, saying "This is getting extremely annoying. The constant racket that these people make is preventing me from sleeping! Give the order to my son Namtar to introduce a deadly flu-type disease that will sicken, weaken and kill them off, in doing so, we can dramatically reduce their numbers". *(3)*

1. *While 1,200 years seems to be what was reported in many of the translated texts, other translations I've read seem to indicate that it may have been 60x1200 or 36,000 years. While I have mixed thoughts about the 1,200 years I used, I chose to go with this amount as it was used by most of the translations I'd read.*
2. *This was a definite No-No in Enlil's eyes, as Enlil seemed to have seen the humans as animals or cattle, regardless of whether they had souls or not. Enlil probably saw the Igigi taking human wives as disgusting behaviour and a poisoning of the Igigi gene pool. Also, once the Igigi had worked out that they were genetically compatible with the new human*

creation, they didn't have to resort to a birth goddess to reproduce anymore and probably felt more independent and less reliant on the Anunnaki control system. With the human chromosomes and DNA being compatible with theirs, they happily took human wives and interbred with them, probably creating yet more unique human-god hybrid beings. I'd be guessing that due to the increasing Igigi DNA being introduced into the human gene pool, the new humans were becoming more similar to the Anunnaki as the "being of the Earth" DNA was slowly being bred out. This may have been seen by some of the higher Anunnaki gods as a future pending threat to their control. One other thing I noticed was there is nowhere in any of the translated texts that mentioned female Igigi, they all seemed to be male labour workers. There may have indeed been female Igigi, however, they were possibly sterile or needed assistance from the birth goddesses to reproduce. This may be extremely significant, as without fertile women the Igigi didn't have any way of naturally and independently reproducing and would have always been under Anunnaki control. Enlil's excuses for wiping out the humans because they were too noisy may have just been a smoke-screen to hide his real fear of losing control. As the Igigi interbred with the humans this made them more independent of their Anunnaki controllers. The Igigi's genetic compatibility with the humans may have been Enlil's and the other Anunnaki gods' real concern.

3. *I went for a flu-type disease here as the symptoms mentioned in the texts I read seemed to indicate a Black Plague or an Ebola outbreak and a deadly flu seemed to cover this.*

The Introduction of Atrahasis and the End of the Plague

Amongst the humans there was one called Atrahasis who was king of the city of Shuruppak *(1)*, Atrahasis was not only extremely intelligent and wise, but also had a friendship relationship with his god Enki. Atrahasis would spend time walking and talking with Enki and Enki enjoyed having various conversations with him.

Figure 16 – Image of Atrahasis, king of the city of Shuruppak situated on the bank of the Euphrates River.

During the plague introduced by Enlil, Atrahasis approached Enki and enquired, "How long will the gods make us suffer with this disease? Will we have to endure it forever?"*(2)* Enki pondered over the question and answered his servant and friend saying, "What you need to do is instruct the elders and senior men to meet at your home and have an official meeting about the problem. As a group, you need to stand strong and forcefully make a noise about the situation all over the land." Enki continued, "Stop worshipping the gods and respecting them, don't pray to your goddesses, however, search for the home of Enlil's son Namtar the creator of the disease and bring him gifts of baked loafs and tasty food offerings. The offering of the gifts and presents will probably make him feel ashamed with what he's done and hopefully he'll stop sickening and killing the people".

Atrahasis did what Enki had suggested and gathered the elders and senior men to his home and told them of Enki's plan. The elders listened to the strategy and did exactly what Enki had suggested. In addition to this, they also built a temple in the city dedicated to Namtar. As discussed in their meeting, they then spread the word of dissatisfaction and distrust of the gods amongst the people. According to the plan, all of the gods, except Namtar, were ignored with no respect expressed. The people stopped visiting the goddesses' temples with food offerings and also stopped praying or requesting anything from them. They did however, proceed to leave offerings for Namtar at his home and he was the only god that was respected and treated well. Namtar was ashamed and embarrassed by the offerings, as he was the only god being noticed by the people. It didn't take long before Namtar decided that enough is enough and stopped the spreading of the disease. With that, the people recovered and the gods were again respected and treated well with the people's offerings.

> 1. *Atrahasis is actually mentioned in the "Sumerian King List" under the name of Ubaru-Tutu as the 8th king, it's also documented that he reigned in Shuruppak for 18,600 years before the flood. This would mean that the people of those days probably lived extended lives compared to the humans of today and possibly why they continued to multiply and over-populate the area. The added wisdom and learnings acquired with the extremely long lives of these humans may have added to the reasons why the higher Anunnaki gods (and especially Enlil) saw them as a threat and this threat contributed towards the decisions made to eliminate them before they became educated and a serious problem to them.*
> 2. *Enki and Atrahasis were obviously aware of what Enlil was doing through his son Namtar. The fact that Enki or Atrahasis*

hadn't done anything until that time indicates that Enlil had full control. It can also be assumed that the human deaths hadn't hit a biblical proportion at that stage. Also, Enki was either scared of going against his brother or he wasn't concerned or planning to do anything about it until Atrahasis asked for help.

Figure 17 – The Sumerian King List on display at the Ashmolean Museum in Oxford, England.

TABLET 2

Enlil Initiates a Famine & Atrahasis Calls on Enki

Everything was fine for a while, though once again, after another 1,200 years or so had passed, the amount of people had increased again to even more than the last time. The city and surrounding lands were again noisy and crowded and once again it came to the point where Enlil started complaining about how the racket was disturbing him. "This is getting ridiculous, there are even more of them than the last time and I'm still being kept awake due to their noise", Enlil said to the great gods while they were in meeting. Enlil continued, "Okay, cut off the food supplies to the people and let there be a shortage of edible vegetation. Order the god, Adad who's in charge of the rains to stop them, so the plants die and food doesn't grow. *(1)* I also want Adad to make the sun and wind scorch the lands and the clouds not to gather so it doesn't rain or shade the area. In addition to this, the wells shall be emptied and access to water from the streams and dams prevented". Adad did as ordered and slowly a drought took hold of the land.

After a few years, having depleted all the food stores, famine hit the land and the people were starving and in pain. The whole situation was horrible, with some of the people resorting to cannibalism to survive. Atrahasis, king and ruler of the people again needed help from his Lord Enki. This time however, Enki had been forbidden by oath to speak to Atrahasis by Enlil and the council. In addition to this, Enki was also far away deep in the underworld of the Abzu. Knowing this and that there was no way he could contact his lord, he walked out of the city each day and wept, but still brought offerings to the gods with the hope that they may change their decision and end the famine. After time, Atrahasis thought of a method to contact Enki and attempted to communicate with him through his dreams. *(2)* He positioned his bed near the river's edge and through a dreaming process approached Enki, pleading for his lord's help with the terrible situation. In the dreaming state Atrahasis inquired, "Lord Enki, why has Adad done this? Why again have the gods made us suffer like this? All the people are starving and dying and some people are even eating each other, no one feels safe. This isn't the happy city it used to be".

1. *Adad seemed to be in charge of the advanced weather modification technology that was used by the gods. I'd assume that it would be something similar to the geoengineering technology we use today.*
2. *Atrahasis used some type of dream communication, possibly a form of telepathy. While this area is missing from the original Atrahasis tablet due to damage, other cuneiform texts that contain sections of the story helped bridge the gaps of the missing sections. These sections of text seemed to indicate that the positioning of his bed next to the water's edge somehow enhanced his ability to contact Enki with the river seeming to aid with the telepathic transmission signal strength. There may be a clue for us here. Someday, we may possibly develop a reliable ESP or telepathic communication technology in the future based on this.*

Enki Responds to Atrahasis' Dream Request

Through his dreams Enki listened *(1)* to what Atrahasis had communicated and was horrified. As he was not able to contact his trusty servant in person due to his oath, Enki instructed a couple of the hairy hero-men *(2)* of the Abzu to contact Atrahasis directly and relay his return message. Like before, Enki suggested the same method be used as when Namtar had sent the plagues over the land and made the people sick with disease. So once again, the elders were gathered in Atrahasis' home and again the same plan was deployed. The elders of the lands organised the erection of a temple to Adad in the city and again the people stopped respecting, making offerings and praying to their gods. Adad was the only god to be treated with respect by the people and they made him food offerings of baked breads and other flour based foods from the very little they had. The people also made a concerted effort to be quiet in the city and the chaotic noise that Enlil was constantly complaining about subsided.

The plan worked, Adad felt extremely ashamed and sorry with what he had been doing and then one morning he arranged for the rains to return. To also help speed up the healing of the people, Enki had organised for the hairy hero-men to collapse one of the god's food storage dams, letting a flood of fish wash over the city and help feed the people. *(3)* Over time, vegetation again grew, the fields were in abundance with crops and the famine had left the people.

1. *I wondered here why Enki didn't respond to Atrahasis in the dream state. It may have been that no communication type was allowed with Enki's oath. This would mean that the other gods (and possibly the humans) were aware of the dreaming communication as well and maybe also used it. Another thought is that he also needed to dispatch the hairy hero-men to participate in the releasing of the fish to feed the people, so used them to also relay his message to Atrahasis.*
2. *Hairy hero-men of the Abzu? This one had me baffled, however, that's what it says. Speculatively you may assume a Neanderthal race or trained great apes, however, these hairy hero-men could apparently speak to relay Enki's message. Primates don't have the vocal systems of humans to communicate, so, I'd assume it was a type of hairy human, possibly a strong worker type that was used in the Abzu.*
3. *It seems that the gods had their own food storage dams where fish were stored for their own consumption. Obviously, the starving people were prevented from getting near to them, or these dams would have long been raided. Now knowing that the gods stored their fish in dedicated dams, I'd also assume the same went for cattle and other livestock which was reserved for the gods.*

When Enlil heard of this he was furious and immediately called a meeting of the gods. Annoyed, insulted and upset he addressed the assembly saying, "We the great Anunna gods all agreed together with the plan. Our father Anu and Adad were to be in charge and the guardians *(1)* of the skies from heaven and the upper regions, while I was to be in charge and guard the earth below. Enki was meant to be in charge of the waters and the happenings in the lower lands of the Abzu and also exercise balance *(2)* in our council. However, he's not only been the creator of mankind, but he's also taught and educated these humans, teaching them our secrets of the heavens. *(3)* In doing so, he has corrupted mankind". Still fuming, Enlil turned to Nusku his high official and said, "Go and fetch Enki, I want him here right away!"

1. *The texts indicate that Adad and Anu watched the skies and upper Earth as guardians. Guardians of what? Would this mean that there were other gods out there that had an interest in Earth and Adad and Anu were merely just the gate keepers? Assuming this, it would also be fair to assume that firstly, Earth was worth guarding and secondly that there were other "gods" that had an interest in the planet.*
2. *It would appear that Enki played an important part in the gods' decisions as he brought "balance" to the gods' meetings. I'd assume that he shared a position similar to a high judge with Enlil and Nintu. The balance Enlil spoke of, was probably given to Enki due to Anu knowing that Enlil might have resorted to bullying tactics on the other Anunnaki gods in council and make erratic and emotionally driven choices that could be detrimental.*
3. *Enlil seemed annoyed that Enki was passing on "secrets of the heavens" to the humans. From an "Ancient Aliens" standpoint, I'd assume that the technologies of the gods were slowly being leaked to the humans. With extended longevity in ancient times and the rapid acquirement of knowledge and*

wisdom due to this, Enlil probably envisaged the growing population of humans as a pending threat. The corrupting of mankind that Enlil referred to was probably due to Enki's persistence in not keeping the humans ignorant. Enlil obviously felt more relaxed when he saw humans as ignorant animal slaves that doted on the gods. Being able to reproduce without any help from the gods and being able to educate and improve with time was obviously a problem for Enlil, and in the council there were obviously others who agreed with him and felt the same way.

Enki was summoned and made to wait in the assembly room with the other gods. He sat there worried about what his brother Enlil was about to say. *(1)* Enlil again addressed the assembly of the gods including his brother Enki, saying, "We the Anunna gods had agreed to our positions. Our father, King Anu and Adad were to guard the heavens, I was to be in charge of the lands and you Enki were supposed to bring balance to council and control the waters and the lower lands". Enlil continued, "Instead, you have overstepped your boundaries brother and defied my orders and given wisdom and knowledge to the people. You've also shamed the gods and made them defy my commands by teaching man to disrespect the gods and their positions". *(2)*

1. *Enki had reason to worry about what his brother had to say. Other ancient cuneiform texts seem to indicate that through council agreement, even Enki may have been sentenced to death for breaking his oath. The oaths that the gods took were extremely binding and Enki obviously knowing why his brother summoned him from the Abzu had reason to be nervous. I'd assume that because Enlil and council's previous plans of killing the humans could be seen to have been diverted by Enlil's own off-spring, Enlil chose not to pursue and prosecute the disobedience of these gods. However, it*

could also be that most of the humans had been eliminated in those times and he was no longer concerned about their numbers.
2. *Enlil again seemed to be very concerned with Enki educating the humans and the wisdom that they seemed to be acquiring. Enlil then continues to say that Enki was teaching the humans to disrespect the gods and their positions. My assumption here is that due to the longevity of the humans and with an educational process in place, the disrespecting of the gods was already happening as the humans started realizing what the really gods were. I've no doubt that the educated humans slowly starting to see through the gods' control methods and motives.*

Enlil Proposes a Flood to Wipe-out Humanity

Enlil continued further saying, "Enki, you caused Namtar to ignore my command and stop his diseases, allowing mankind to return to health. In addition to this, you were then the cause for Adad to cease stopping the rains and the famine I arranged was ended. However, not only did you stop the drought, but you also arranged for a flood of fish to feed the people from Anunnaki stocks. You took it upon yourself to go against the will of the gods. The humans that you created were due to the death of an Anunnaki god, you participated in the slaughter of him and the end of his intelligence, *(1)* due to this and as punishment I will now command you to participate with the destruction of this human creation." Enlil proceeded to address Enki, "You Enki, have been supporting the wrong plan and will use your knowledge and control of the diked waters and mooring poles to flood and destroy mankind from the land. *(2)* In front of the Anunna gods you will swear to do this".

Annoyed, Enki abruptly stood up and raised his voice responding to Enlil's vicious command. Facing the assembly he aggressively answered, "Why would I agree to make such an oath and use my powers against my own people? What is this flood my brother speaks of? I don't know what he's talking about." Having the assembly's full attention Enki continued, "This type of destruction and murder is my brother Enlil's type of work and I refuse to participate! If Enlil wants to cause a flood, let him organise his own people to do it and not me! His son Ninurta is capable of doing this, so why doesn't he command him to loosen the mooring poles and make the dikes overflow to flood the city instead of me?"

The assembly listened to Enki and agreed that he shouldn't have to be directly responsible for the flooding of the city and killing the humans. They did however decide that even though the flood wasn't to be done by his hand, he should still be sworn by oath to not repeat the plan to a living soul. The assembly then agreed to Enlil's evil deed of the annihilation of mankind.

1. *The fact that it was not just the organised death of an Anunnaki god (remember it was Enlil that called for Geshtu's execution as an example to the Igigi) but also the end of his intelligence that makes me wonder if this indeed meant that all soul knowledge was lost. Does it mean that the soul would not be recycled as in reincarnation or just that the accumulated knowledge that the young god had acquired in his life existence would be lost? This would therefore mean that the knowledge acquired by the gods in their lives was either stored somehow or maybe transferred to other god bodies or beings, which was obviously, sadly not the case with poor Geshtu. I've pondered over this "intelligence being lost" statement quite a bit and as this is mentioned a number of times in different places in the Atrahasis text, I'd assume it must be of some importance.*
2. *It's pretty logical to assume that this was to be a localized flood and not a global one as reported in the case of the Genesis flood with Noah. My assumption is that the mooring poles and diked waters Enlil refers to were part of the ancient canal systems from the Euphrates River that still partly exists today. Enki obviously had control of the dammed waters and I*

assume that they were probably higher up the hill sides, with the Shuruppak city in the valley. I can just imagine the catastrophe if the huge dam wall were to break flooding the populace in the valley. The tsunami of water would be immediate, with the strength of the rush of water alone enough to kill everything in its path totally destroying everything on the lower plains and in the valley.

TABLET 3

Enki Warns Atrahasis of the Pending Flood

Now Atrahasis sought his master Enki, hunting for him day and night. As Enki had been forced to swear an oath of silence he could not speak to any person of the pending catastrophe, so he refused to answer Atrahasis and deliberately avoided him. Instead of addressing Atrahasis directly, Enki decided to approach him in a dream instructing him to wait outside his bedroom at his temple and he would reveal the troubled consequences that were planned. Peering out of his bedroom window Enki then waited and watched Atrahasis arrive. When he was sure Atrahasis was waiting outside on the other side of his bedroom wall, he directly addressed the wall from the inside. With a loud and stern voice he instructed, "Reed wall, pay attention to all the words I say!" *(1)* Confused, Atrahasis placed his ear next to the reed wall and in a loud voice responded and asked, "Lord Enki, what is the meaning of the dream and how will I overcome the consequences planned?" Enki, now knowing that his faithful servant and friend was on the other side of the reed wall then continued to speak, saying, "Reed wall, I have been forbidden by oath to speak to a living soul and will continue to speak to you while I'm in my bedroom. Reed wall, you need to listen and pay attention to all of my words and take note"

Enki continued speaking to the reed wall with Atrahasis on the other side of it, saying, "Flee your house and dismantle it to build a sealed boat of considerable size. You need to forego all worldly possessions and flee for your life. The boat that you build needs to be roofed and the roof sealed to not let in a single bit of light from the sun. The boat also needs to be strong and sturdy and covered in bitumen tar to seal it from water coming in from all directions. I will shower on the boat at a later date stocks of birds and fish". Enki opened up a water clock and while filling it continued speaking in a raised voice to the reed wall explaining that a seven day flood was about to happen and that the water clock should be observed.

1. *Addressing the reed wall and not a "living soul" was Enki's way of keeping his oath. His future planned argument (if needed) was probably it wasn't his fault that someone happened to be on the other side of the wall while he was addressing it. The swearing by oath not to tell anyone or a "living soul" was Enki's way of yet again defying his brother. This part of the ancient texts is thought to be one of the biggest jokes ever in these sad circumstances and was the reason that the total annihilation of mankind was said to have been prevented.*

Atrahasis Builds a Boat and Escapes the Flood

Understanding Enki's warning, Atrahasis sped off and gathered the Elders of Shuruppak to his home. Speaking clearly, he addressed them saying, "My god Enki does not agree with your god Enlil, the two of them are constantly bickering and angry with each other. Since I've always supported Enki I've now been told by Enlil to leave his city and move down to the Abzu and live in Enki's land and never set foot in Enlil's lands again. *(1)* I need help to build a boat to take me there".

The elders listened to what Atrahasis had said and called together carpenters and various other workers to assist in the building of their king's boat on the edge of the Euphrates river bank. The rich men provided equipment and workers, the poor men provided their labour and carried the equipment. When the boat was sealed at its completion, pure animals were brought to it and a few were slaughtered and prepared for food. The rest of the cattle, sheep and birds were stored on-board for their king's journey. Satisfied that his boat was built in time, Atrahasis then threw a huge feast for the city of Shuruppak to celebrate and there was an abundance of food and drink for everyone. While the citizens of Shuruppak were eating and drinking, Atrahasis couldn't sit still and was constantly moving between the boat and the feast. Guilt ridden, upset and heartbroken with what he'd done and also what was about to occur he was sickened to the extent that he was vomiting bile. *(2)* Knowing what was about to happen, Atrahasis gathered up his family members and brought them on-board as the weather slowly started changing. With the livestock and his family safely on-board Atrahasis cut the mooring ropes and returned to the boat. He climbed on-board and closed the main door and with buckets of pitch he sealed the boat from the inside.

1. *This was an outright lie that Atrahasis felt was necessary to bestow on the good nature of his people to save himself. Saying what he did, and not even warning the people was bad enough. As we see, he not only fails to offer a hint of a warning, but even employs the city people's help to make his getaway craft, leaving them all to perish.*
2. *I think I'd be more than guilt ridden and be vomiting bile, imagine having the knowledge that you were the reason of mankind's demise on your conscious. I still can't see why Atrahasis didn't warn his people of the upcoming catastrophe and recommend that they "head for the hills" or build boats for themselves. There was no mention in the texts that he was sworn to secrecy to Enki about mentioning the planned disaster.*

Figure 18 – A possible depiction of Atrahasis escaping the flood.

Enlil's Flood Kills Mankind and Enki Exposes Nintu's Guilt

As commanded, Adad caused the weather to roar in the clouds and the gods could hear the noise from their safe place. *(1)* While the winds roared and raged, the storm cut into the dykes breaking them like clay pots. The uncontrollable flood then rushed out over the people like an army of water. The sun was blacked out by the storm and the wind screamed like an eagle. In the complete darkness of the storm and in the onslaught of water, no one could recognise each other in the catastrophe. Dead bodies of men, women and children floated on the water.

Watching this happen, Enki was extremely upset and beside himself to see the death of his beloved people and turned to his sister Nintu saying, "Birth goddess, creator of mankind and his destiny, you have assisted with this destruction of all people." Nintu was scared and also upset as she wailed and gnawed her lips in agony waiting thirsty and hungry for the storm to end. Weeping, Nintu spoke, saying, "Let the day grow dark and let it turn to gloom. How did Enlil convince me to agree with him and the other gods to help with this annihilation? Was Enlil so strong that he forced me to agree to this? Did he make my speech confused? No! It is of my own doing! My children that I created are dead because of me and I've made no effort to save them as they wash up upon the shores like dead dragon flies. Due to this and my choice to remain silent, I now have to live in grief regretting this for the rest of my days. Shall I go and live with Anu in heaven in a house that has everything I need? Where has Anu gone, the chief decision maker of his sons that heeded his every command? Inadvertently, by giving them this control he brought the flood on himself!" *(2)* Nintu continued to wail and the other gods joined her and also wailed for their land. Uncomfortable and huddled together, Nintu longed for the taste of beer again and like the other gods was suffering from hunger and had lips agonising with thirst. For seven days and seven nights the great Anunna gods sat huddled together, thirsty, scared and with pains of hunger they waited the storm out. When the seventh day had past, the earth fell silent and the sun came out.

1. *There's no indication in the texts where the "safe place" was. It can be assumed that they had a retreat either in a cave or building further up near the top of one of the hills or mountains. Whatever it was, they could definitely witness the power of Adad's storm from where they were.*
2. *It's interesting here that Nintu moves the blame onto her father for giving full control to Enlil and the gods. It may be that as Anu was also a warrior and close to his son Enlil that he shared his son's dislike and fear of the humans.
Regardless of this, Nintu obviously wasn't scared to blame her father, the king, in front of the other gods.*

Atrahasis Exits the Boat

Hearing the silence, Atrahasis removed some of the pitch and opened a small window on the top of his sealed boat and the brilliance of the sun shone in. He then took a raven and released it through the small opening and waited. It didn't return. Slowly, the occupants of the boat felt the waters receding and the boat stopped moving, gently settling on firm land amongst some mountains. After waiting for further movement and when convinced there wasn't any, King Atrahasis dropped open the main door of his sealed vessel and let the animals and his family out. Safely on dry land they all took deep breaths of fresh air and relaxed, enjoying the warmth of the sun on their skin. Thankful for his lord Enki's help, Atrahasis organised the slaughter of one of the cattle and prepared a burnt offering to his god. The smell of the cooked meat filled the air and the gods were drawn to it like flies. *(1)*

When the gods had eaten their fill, Nintu got up and addressed the great Anunnu gods, blaming them for the catastrophe saying, "Whatever came over Anu to agree to Enlil's plan of devastation and agree to the destruction of mankind? *(2)* What kind of decision maker instead of sorting out a problem situation, chooses to rather resolve it by annihilation? The happy faces of our children are now gone forever."

> 1. *It's interesting that the gods were in smelling distance of the cooking meat. Does this mean that they were waiting the storm out at the top of the same mountain that the sealed boat settled on? If the boat was moored on the Euphrates River as mentioned in the texts and with the enormous avalanche of water that hit it, logical assumption would be that the sealed vessel would speed down the Euphrates River at great velocity, probably ending up in the Persian Gulf. The fact that the gods were so near to where Atrahasis' vessel settled appears strange to me.*

2. *Nintu again blames her father, King Anu, in front of the other gods. She obviously understands her brother Enlil's character, but can't understand why her father would agree to Enlil's evil plan and questions his judgement as a leader. This to me seems like a personal escape plan to help clear her own conscience for not supporting Enki.*

Enlil & Enki's Fury

Enki quietly went down to the water's edge and seeing the bodies of his people on the shore wept in sorrow with the carnage Enlil had caused. Nintu slowly moved to join her brother, turning to the watching gods she said, "Enki's pain is also mine and from now on my destiny is as his and I will wear a dragon fly pendant around my neck forever to remind me of this".

It was then that Enlil and his father Anu arrived. *(1)* Seeing Atrahasis' boat, Enlil was furious with the other gods. In a furious state he addressed them shouting, "We the Anunna gods had an agreement and made an oath. How did this life escape from and survive the catastrophe?" Anu then spoke up and answered Enlil, "Who but Enki would do this and disclose the order?" Seeing there was no getting out of the situation and still very upset, Enki aggressively jumped up and shouted back at Enlil, "Yes, it was me who defied you all and decided to preserve life! Punish me as you will, but I have made a conscience decision and have vented my feelings to you. Where is the logic of killing everything that lives? Yes, it was me who saved mankind and I did it to save not only them, but also for your sakes."

Feeling the power of his brother's wrath and fearing that Enki would be supported by the other gods, Enlil relaxed and backed down. Not knowing of the previous discussions between the gods and also Nintu's pledge to support Enki before his and Anu's arrival, he answered Enki saying, "Okay Enki, let's see if the birth goddess, our sister, Nintu agrees with you. I'm happy for the two of you to discuss the issue and I'll go along with whatever Nintu decides." Enki then turned and addressed his sister and with a softened voice said, "Nintu, you are the birth goddess. The creator of destinies of the people and of all the gods, whatever you now say will be made so. I feel we should make a bond between Heaven and Earth and also make Enlil swear to behold it as he made us swear to his oath."

1. *The question that needs to be asked here is, where did Anu and Enlil arrive from? They obviously weren't with the other gods in their hide-away from the storm, otherwise King Anu would have heard what Nintu had said about him and his leadership. Both King Anu and Enlil would have also been aware of Nintu's pledge to support Enki.*

Nintu Makes Enlil Swear an Oath

Nodding in agreement, Nintu sprung up and immediately drew a circle pattern on the ground in some spilt flour. *(1)* Adding a heaped mound of it in the centre of the circle she instructed Enlil to stand on it and swear a bond between Heaven and Earth. True to his word and without question, Enlil stood on the heaped flour in the circle and swore to withhold the bond between heaven and earth and never again to harm the people of the land. He also included his own addition, adding that the Anunnaki and Igigi will never again be allowed to cohabit and breed with the children of the humans. *(2)*

The Priestess-Hood and Procreation Ruling is Introduced

Nintu then added, that among the people one third of the woman born will be sworn to priestess-hood and serve the temples of the gods as priestesses and high priestesses. These priestesses will be respected by all and it will be unacceptable by law for a man to interfere with them. The majority of the classes of priestesses will also remain childless, with any children that may be born to them to be considered as nameless and also without a family name. Nintu also said that there should be amongst the people, a woman that snatches a girl baby from the woman who bore it without a husband. *(3)* This woman will then introduce the infant girl to a high priestess where she will be trained from birth to become a priestess. Nintu finally added that the terrible story of the great flood and the survival of the human race should be written down to be remembered forever and enthusiastically praised in song and verse for all to hear. *(4)*

1. *I've never managed to work out what the significance of the heap of flour with a circle drawn around it was meant to be, and also why Enlil was instructed to stand in the circle on top of the mound of flour? It could possibly be a symbol of oath that the Anunnaki used in front of other gods, or it's possible that the true meaning was lost in the cuneiform translation (maybe still to be discovered). I'd assume that writing in flour or in meal like Nintu did to document the first child birth, was probably a way of recording the incident. The circle in flour may mean that the swearing of the oath by Enlil was recorded as a treaty or as a contract would be.*
2. *The section about preventing the humans breeding with the gods was not part of the oath that Nintu had instructed Enlil to swear to. It would appear that Enlil sneaked this part in as if it was Nintu's idea. As mentioned previously, if Enlil saw humans as animals, the thought that the Igigi and Anunnu gods were procreating with them probably sickened him immensely. Even though the mating of humans and gods didn't cease at that point (as we had Gilgamesh and many other demi-gods that later came to be born from god and human unions). Enlil must have felt satisfied that he'd managed to add this little bit into his oath to Nintu and the other gods.*
3. *There is no mention of what happens to male babies born out of wedlock, as only female babies were to be snatched away. I can't see that the male babies would be cruelly left to die, so assume*

that they were either made into eunuchs to also serve in the temples, or left with the unwed mother and also remained nameless.

4. *Well… It looks like Nintu got her way. Here I am re-writing the whole story to share for everyone to read. I'm not sure if I'm up to the verse and song bit though so my adaptation of the story in print will have to surmise.*

THANKS FOR READING ☺

ACKNOWLEDGEMENTS AND SOME POINTS TO PONDER ON:

Benjamin R. Foster: Before the Muses: An Anthology of Akkadian Literature (Volume 1 – Archaic, Classical, Mature). Atrahasis extract available at:
https://docs.google.com/viewer?a=v&pid=sites&srcid=c3RmcmFuY2lzc2Nob29sLm9yZ3xiYWJ5bG9ufGd4OjI0YjE4YjlhYWRjOWE0YTg

James B. Pritchard: Ancient Near Eastern Texts – Relating to the Old Testament

George Smith: The Chaldean Account of Genesis

W.G Lambert & A.R Millard: Atra-Hasis – The Babylonian Story of the Flood with the Sumerian flood Story

Samuel Noah Kramer: Reflections on the Mesopotamian Flood (Available to read at:
https://www.penn.museum/sites/expedition/reflections-on-the-mesopotamian-flood/)

Stephanie Dalley: Myths from Mesopotamia: Creation, the Flood, Gilgamesh, and Others. (Atrahasis extract available at: http://www.gatewaystobabylon.com/myths/texts/enki/atraha1.htm)
https://www.bibliotecapleyades.net/serpents_dragons/boulay03e_a.htm

John A. Halloran: Sumerian Lexicon (Online version available at: https://www.sumerian.org/sumerlex.htm)

PHOTOS AND ILLUSTRATIONS

Front Cover: The cover photo is the same shown in Figure 5 but with a slight modification. The original photo was modified by JustinQ7 by adding a black background.

Figure 1: Estimated Dates of Ancient and Historical Writings (Diagram by M Lewis)

Figure 2: Noah's Ark (Wikimedia Commons, Public Domain by Knut). Photo can be found at: https://commons.wikimedia.org/wiki/File:Flanell-Noa1a.JPG . Photo attributed to: https://nn.wikipedia.org/wiki/Brukar:Knut

Figure 3: Baalbek Platform - Large Megalith Stones (Wikimedia Commons, Public domain by Dumas). Photo can be found at: https://www.loc.gov/pictures/item/2004667860/ Photo attributed to:

https://commons.wikimedia.org/wiki/File:...)es_Ciclopeenes_-_Dumas_LCCN2004667860.jpg

Figure 4: Baalbek - Lone Stone left in Quarry (Flickr – Public domain by Copyright Holder, Caroline Granycome). Photo can be found at: https://www.flickr.com/photos/cgranycome/7162796619/in/photostream/ . Caroline Granycome's profile can be found at: https://www.flickr.com/people/cgranycome/

Figure 5: Atrahasis Tablets in British Museum ME78941 (Wikimedia Commons, free use granted into the Public Domain by jack1956). Photo can be found at: https://commons.wikimedia.org/wiki/File:Bm-epic-g.jpg . jack1956's profile can be found at: https://en.wikipedia.org/wiki/User:Jack1956

Figure 6: Cuneiform Symbol for Anu (Wikipedia - Public domain by Geoff Richards). The photo can be found at: https://commons.wikimedia.org/wiki/File:Cuneiform_sumer_dingir.svg . Geoff Richards' profile can be found at: https://en.wikipedia.org/wiki/User:Qef

Figure 7: Enlil & Ninlil (Wikimedia Commons – Released into the Public Domain by author Roberto.Amerighi). The photo can be found at: https://commons.wikimedia.org/wiki/File:Enlil_e_Ninlil.jpg Robert Amerighi's profile can be found at: https://commons.wikimedia.org/wiki/User:Roberto.Amerighi

Figure 8: The Adda Seal in the British Museum (Wikimedia Commons - Public Domain and attributed to "The British Museum Collections"). The photo can be found at: https://en.wikipedia.org/wiki/File:Ea_(Babilonian)_-_EnKi_(Sumerian).jpg . The British Museum's Collections profile can be found at: https://commons.wikimedia.org/wiki/Category:Collections_of_the_British_Museum

Figure 9: Okavango Delta 1 (Courtesy of Google Earth: Approximate Co-Ordinates -19.824346 21.714989). Google Earth can be downloaded free at:

https://www.google.com/earth/download/gep/agree.html Permissions Page can be found here: https://www.google.com/permissions/geoguidelines/ Attributed to "Google Earth" is printed in the bottom right of the image.

Figure 10: Okavango Delta 2 (Courtesy of Google Earth: Approximate Co-Ordinates -19.824346 21.714989). Google Earth can be downloaded free at: https://www.google.com/earth/download/gep/agree.html Permissions Page can be found here: https://www.google.com/permissions/geoguidelines/ Attributed to "Google Earth" is printed in the bottom right of the image.

Figure 11: Okavango Delta 3 (Courtesy of Google Earth: Approximate Co-Ordinates -19.824346 21.714989). Google Earth can be downloaded free from here: https://www.google.com/earth/download/gep/agree.html Permissions Page can be found here: https://www.google.com/permissions/geoguidelines/ Attributed to "Google Earth" is printed in the bottom right of the image.

Figure 12: Nintu in University of Chicago, USA (Wikimedia Commons – Released into the Public Domain with No Restrictions by Daderot). The photo can be found at: https://commons.wikimedia.org/wiki/File:Female_worshipper_with_tufted_dress_and_wrapped_headdress,_Khafajah,_Nintu_Temple_VII,_Early_Dynastic_period,_2600-2500_BC,_gypsum_-_Oriental_Institute_Museum,_University_of_Chicago_-_DSC07453.JPG Daderot's profile can be found at: https://commons.wikimedia.org/wiki/User:Daderot

Figure 13: Inanna (Queen of the night) (Wikimedia Commons and released into the Public Domain by BabelStone). The photo can be found at: https://commons.wikimedia.org/wiki/File:British_Museum_Queen_of_the_Night.jpg Bablestone's profile can be found at: https://commons.wikimedia.org/wiki/User:BabelStone

Figure 14: Human + Chimp Chromosomes (Wikimedia Commons by JWSchmidt - Free to use, modify. GNU licence). Photo can be found here: https://commons.wikimedia.org/wiki/File:Humanchimpchromosomes.png JWSchmidt's profile can be found at: https://en.wikipedia.org/wiki/User:JWSchmidt

Figure 15: Shu-ilishus Cylinder Seal (Wikimedia Commons - Public Domain and the original author is listed as unknown). Photo can be found here: https://commons.wikimedia.org/wiki/File:Sigillo_su_un_cilindro_di_Shu-ilishus.jpg While the original author is unknown, the photo was uploaded by Roberto Amerighi. Robert's profile can be found here: https://commons.wikimedia.org/wiki/User:Roberto.Amerighi

Figure 16: Atrahasis, the person (Wikimedia Commons – Public Domain). The photo can be found at: https://commons.wikimedia.org/wiki/File:Sargon_of_Akkad.jpg and the details of the author's profile can be found here: https://commons.wikimedia.org/wiki/User:Shakko

Figure 17: Sumerian King List (Wikimedia Commons – Released into the Public Domain by Taiwania Justo). The photo can be found at: https://commons.wikimedia.org/wiki/File:Sumeriankinglist.jpg

Taiwania Justo's profile details can be found here: https://commons.wikimedia.org/wiki/User:Taiwania_Justo , here: https://zh.wikipedia.org/wiki/User:%E4%BF%9E%E7%A3%8A and here: https://home.yulei.org/

Figure 18: Image from page 101 of 'Babel and Bible' 1906 (Public domain – No Known Copyright Restrictions). The photo can be found at: https://visualhunt.com/f2/photo/14579921717/3e6db109f9/ Source is listed as flickr and author as Internet Archive Book Images. Found on flickr at:
https://www.flickr.com/photos/internetarchivebookimages/14579921717/

ABOUT THE AUTHOR

Steven Q has been studying ancient civilisations and writings for a number of years and has developed a passion for discovering our ancient past. Understanding the past helps to understand the present.

Steven has a website http://www.theworldaccordingtostevenq.com where he discusses various topics close to his heart.

If you have would like to contact Steven, please feel free to email him at: stevenq7@hotmail.com

Made in United States
North Haven, CT
04 May 2024